Singapore MATH

Appropriate for Students in
GRADE 3

70 Must-Know WORD PROBLEMS

Thinking Kids®
An imprint of Carson-Dellosa Publishing LLC
Greensboro, North Carolina

Visit *carsondellosa.com* for correlations to Common Core, state, national, and Canadian provincial standards.

Copyright © 2009 Singapore Asia Publishers PTE LTD.

Thinking Kids®
An imprint of Carson-Dellosa Publishing LLC
PO Box 35665
Greensboro, NC 27425 USA

ISBN 978-0-7682-4012-2
11-195207784

INTRODUCTION TO SINGAPORE MATH

Welcome to Singapore Math! The math curriculum in Singapore has been recognized worldwide for its excellence in producing students highly skilled in mathematics. Students in Singapore have ranked at the top in the world in mathematics on the *Trends in International Mathematics and Science Study* (TIMSS) in 1993, 1995, 2003, and 2008. Because of this, Singapore Math has gained in interest and popularity in the United States.

Singapore Math curriculum aims to help students develop the necessary math concepts and process skills for everyday life and to provide students with the ability to formulate, apply, and solve problems. Mathematics in the Singapore Primary (Elementary) Curriculum cover fewer topics but in greater depth. Key math concepts are introduced and built-on to reinforce various mathematical ideas and thinking. Students in Singapore are typically one grade level ahead of students in the United States.

The following pages provide examples of the various math problem types and skill sets taught in Singapore.

At an elementary level, some simple mathematical skills can help students understand mathematical principles. These skills are the counting-on, counting-back, and crossing-out methods. Note that these methods are most useful when the numbers are small.

1. The Counting-On Method

Used for addition of two numbers. Count on in 1s with the help of a picture or number line.

$$7 + 4 = \mathbf{11}$$

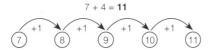

2. The Counting-Back Method

Used for subtraction of two numbers. Count back in 1s with the help of a picture or number line.

$$16 - 3 = \mathbf{13}$$

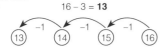

3. The Crossing-Out Method

Used for subtraction of two numbers. Cross out the number of items to be taken away. Count the remaining ones to find the answer.

$$20 - 12 = \mathbf{8}$$

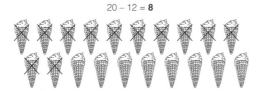

A **number bond** shows the relationship in a simple addition or subtraction problem. The number bond is based on the concept "part-part-whole." This concept is useful in teaching simple addition and subtraction to young children.

To find a whole, students must add the two parts.
To find a part, students must subtract the other part from the whole.

The different types of number bonds are illustrated below.

1. Number Bond (single digits)

3 (part) + 6 (part) = **9** (whole)

9 (whole) − 3 (part) = **6** (part)

9 (whole) − 6 (part) = **3** (part)

2. Addition Number Bond (single digits)

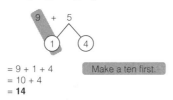

= 9 + 1 + 4   Make a ten first.
= 10 + 4
= **14**

3. Addition Number Bond (double and single digits)

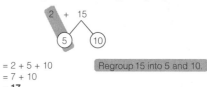

= 2 + 5 + 10   Regroup 15 into 5 and 10.
= 7 + 10
= **17**

4. Subtraction Number Bond (double and single digits)

10 − 7 = 3
3 + 2 = **5**

5. Subtraction Number Bond (double digits)

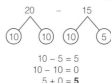

10 − 5 = 5
10 − 10 = 0
5 + 0 = **5**

Students should understand that multiplication is repeated addition and that division is the grouping of all items into equal sets.

1. Repeated Addition (Multiplication)

Mackenzie eats 2 rolls a day. How many rolls does she eat in 5 days?

$$2 + 2 + 2 + 2 + 2 = 10$$
$$5 \times 2 = 10$$

She eats **10** rolls in 5 days.

2. The Grouping Method (Division)

Mrs. Lee makes 14 sandwiches. She gives all the sandwiches equally to 7 friends. How many sandwiches does each friend receive?

$$14 \div 7 = 2$$

Each friend receives **2** sandwiches.

One of the basic but essential math skills students should acquire is to perform the 4 operations of whole numbers and fractions. Each of these methods is illustrated below.

1. The Adding-Without-Regrouping Method

```
  H  T  O
  3  2  1        O: Ones
+ 5  6  8        T: Tens
--------
  8  8  9        H: Hundreds
```

Since no regrouping is required, add the digits in each place value accordingly.

2. The Adding-by-Regrouping Method

```
  H  T  O
  ¹4  9  2       O: Ones
+  1  5  3       T: Tens
--------
  6  4  5        H: Hundreds
```

In this example, regroup 14 tens into 1 hundred 4 tens.

3. The Adding-by-Regrouping-Twice Method

$$\begin{array}{ccc} H & T & O \\ ^1 2 & ^1 8 & 6 \\ + 3 & 6 & 5 \\ \hline 6 & 5 & 1 \end{array}$$

O: Ones
T: Tens
H: Hundreds

Regroup twice in this example.
First, regroup 11 ones into 1 ten 1 one.
Second, regroup 15 tens into 1 hundred 5 tens.

4. The Subtracting-Without-Regrouping Method

$$\begin{array}{ccc} H & T & O \\ 7 & 3 & 9 \\ - 3 & 2 & 5 \\ \hline 4 & 1 & 4 \end{array}$$

O: Ones
T: Tens
H: Hundreds

Since no regrouping is required, subtract the digits in each place value accordingly.

5. The Subtracting-by-Regrouping Method

$$\begin{array}{ccc} H & T & O \\ 5 & ^7 8 & ^{11} 1 \\ - 2 & 4 & 7 \\ \hline 3 & 3 & 4 \end{array}$$

O: Ones
T: Tens
H: Hundreds

In this example, students cannot subtract 7 ones from 1 one. So, regroup the tens and ones. Regroup 8 tens 1 one into 7 tens 11 ones.

6. The Subtracting-by-Regrouping-Twice Method

$$\begin{array}{ccc} H & T & O \\ ^7 8 & ^9 0 & ^{10} 0 \\ - 5 & 9 & 3 \\ \hline 2 & 0 & 7 \end{array}$$

O: Ones
T: Tens
H: Hundreds

In this example, students cannot subtract 3 ones from 0 ones and 9 tens from 0 tens. So, regroup the hundreds, tens, and ones. Regroup 8 hundreds into 7 hundreds 9 tens 10 ones.

7. The Multiplying-Without-Regrouping Method

$$\begin{array}{cc} T & O \\ 2 & 4 \\ \times & 2 \\ \hline 4 & 8 \end{array}$$

O: Ones
T: Tens

Since no regrouping is required, multiply the digit in each place value by the multiplier accordingly.

8. The Multiplying-With-Regrouping Method

$$\begin{array}{ccc} H & T & O \\ ^1 3 & ^2 4 & 9 \\ \times & & 3 \\ \hline 1, 0 & 4 & 7 \end{array}$$

O: Ones
T: Tens
H: Hundreds

In this example, regroup 27 ones into 2 tens 7 ones, and 14 tens into 1 hundred 4 tens.

9. The Dividing-Without-Regrouping Method

$$\begin{array}{r} 2\ 4\ 1 \\ 2\overline{)4\ 8\ 2} \\ \underline{-4} \\ 8 \\ \underline{-8} \\ 2 \\ \underline{-2} \\ 0 \end{array}$$

Since no regrouping is required, divide the digit in each place value by the divisor accordingly.

10. The Dividing-With-Regrouping Method

$$\begin{array}{r} 1\ 6\ 6 \\ 5\overline{)8\ 3\ 0} \\ \underline{-5} \\ 3\ 3 \\ \underline{-3\ 0} \\ 3\ 0 \\ \underline{-3\ 0} \\ 0 \end{array}$$

In this example, regroup 3 hundreds into 30 tens and add 3 tens to make 33 tens. Regroup 3 tens into 30 ones.

11. The Addition-of-Fractions Method

$$\frac{1 \times 2}{6 \times 2} + \frac{1 \times 3}{4 \times 3} = \frac{2}{12} + \frac{3}{12} = \frac{5}{12}$$

Always remember to make the denominators common before adding the fractions.

12. The Subtraction-of-Fractions Method

$$\frac{1 \times 5}{2 \times 5} - \frac{1 \times 2}{5 \times 2} = \frac{5}{10} - \frac{2}{10} = \frac{3}{10}$$

Always remembers to make the denominators common before subtracting the fractions.

13. The Multiplication-of-Fractions Method

$$\frac{^1 3}{5} \times \frac{1}{9 _3} = \frac{1}{15}$$

When the numerator and the denominator have a common multiple, reduce them to their lowest fractions.

14. The Division-of-Fractions Method

$$\frac{7}{9} \div \frac{1}{6} = \frac{7}{9 _3} \times \frac{6 ^2}{1} = \frac{14}{3} = 4\frac{2}{3}$$

When dividing fractions, first change the division sign (÷) to the multiplication sign (×). Then, switch the numerator and denominator of the fraction on the right hand side. Multiply the fractions in the usual way.

Model drawing is an effective strategy used to solve math word problems. It is a visual representation of the information in word problems using bar units. By drawing the models, students will know of the variables given in the problem, the variables to find, and even the methods used to solve the problem.

Drawing models is also a versatile strategy. It can be applied to simple word problems involving addition, subtraction, multiplication, and division. It can also be applied to word problems related to fractions, decimals, percentage, and ratio.

The use of models also trains students to think in an algebraic manner, which uses symbols for representation.

The different types of bar models used to solve word problems are illustrated below.

1. The model that involves addition

Melissa has 50 blue beads and 20 red beads. How many beads does she have altogether?

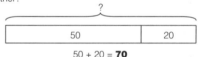

50 + 20 = **70**

2. The model that involves subtraction

Ben and Andy have 90 toy cars. Andy has 60 toy cars. How many toy cars does Ben have?

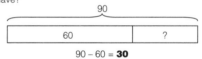

90 − 60 = **30**

3. The model that involves comparison

Mr. Simons has 150 magazines and 110 books in his study. How many more magazines than books does he have?

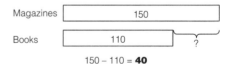

150 − 110 = **40**

4. The model that involves two items with a difference

A pair of shoes costs $109. A leather bag costs $241 more than the pair of shoes. How much is the leather bag?

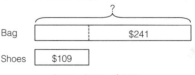

$109 + $241 = **$350**

5. The model that involves multiples

Mrs. Drew buys 12 apples. She buys 3 times as many oranges as apples. She also buys 3 times as many cherries as oranges. How many pieces of fruit does she buy altogether?

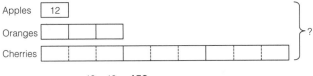

$$13 \times 12 = \textbf{156}$$

6. The model that involves multiples and difference

There are 15 students in Class A. There are 5 more students in Class B than in Class A. There are 3 times as many students in Class C than in Class A. How many students are there altogether in the three classes?

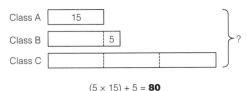

$$(5 \times 15) + 5 = \textbf{80}$$

7. The model that involves creating a whole

Ellen, Giselle, and Brenda bake 111 muffins. Giselle bakes twice as many muffins as Brenda. Ellen bakes 9 fewer muffins than Giselle. How many muffins does Ellen bake?

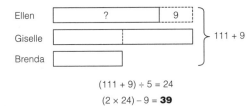

$$(111 + 9) \div 5 = 24$$
$$(2 \times 24) - 9 = \textbf{39}$$

8. The model that involves sharing

There are 183 tennis balls in Basket A and 97 tennis balls in Basket B. How many tennis balls must be transferred from Basket A to Basket B so that both baskets contain the same number of tennis balls?

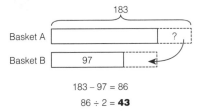

$$183 - 97 = 86$$
$$86 \div 2 = \textbf{43}$$

9. The model that involves fractions

George had 355 marbles. He lost $\frac{1}{5}$ of the marbles and gave $\frac{1}{4}$ of the remaining marbles to his brother. How many marbles did he have left?

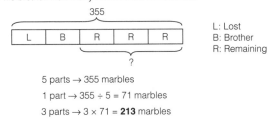

L: Lost
B: Brother
R: Remaining

5 parts → 355 marbles
1 part → 355 ÷ 5 = 71 marbles
3 parts → 3 × 71 = **213** marbles

10. The model that involves ratio

Aaron buys a tie and a belt. The prices of the tie and belt are in the ratio 2 : 5. If both items cost $539,

(a) what is the price of the tie?

(b) what is the price of the belt?

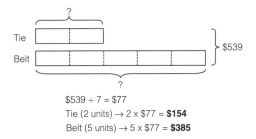

$539 ÷ 7 = $77
Tie (2 units) → 2 x $77 = **$154**
Belt (5 units) → 5 x $77 = **$385**

11. The model that involves comparison of fractions

Jack's height is $\frac{2}{3}$ of Leslie's height. Leslie's height is $\frac{3}{4}$ of Lindsay's height. If Lindsay is 160 cm tall, find Jack's height and Leslie's height.

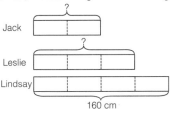

1 unit → 160 ÷ 4 = 40 cm

Leslie's height (3 units) → 3 × 40 = **120 cm**

Jack's height (2 units) → 2 × 40 = **80 cm**

Thinking skills and strategies are important in mathematical problem solving. These skills are applied when students think through the math problems to solve them. Below are some commonly used thinking skills and strategies applied in mathematical problem solving.

1. Comparing

Comparing is a form of thinking skill that students can apply to identify similarities and differences.

When comparing numbers, look carefully at each digit before deciding if a number is greater or less than the other. Students might also use a number line for comparison when there are more numbers.

Example:

3 is greater than 2 but smaller than 7.

2. Sequencing

A sequence shows the order of a series of numbers. *Sequencing* is a form of thinking skill that requires students to place numbers in a particular order. There are many terms in a sequence. The terms refer to the numbers in a sequence.

To place numbers in a correct order, students must first find a rule that generates the sequence. In a simple math sequence, students can either add or subtract to find the unknown terms in the sequence.

Example: Find the 7th term in the sequence below.

1,	4,	7,	10,	13,	16	?
1st term	2nd term	3rd term	4th term	5th term	6th term	7th term

Step 1:   This sequence is in an increasing order.

Step 2:   4 − 1 = 3   7 − 4 = 3
           The difference between two consecutive terms is 3.

Step 3:   16 + 3 = 19
           The 7th term is **19**.

3. Visualization

Visualization is a problem solving strategy that can help students visualize a problem through the use of physical objects. Students will play a more active role in solving the problem by manipulating these objects.

The main advantage of using this strategy is the mobility of information in the process of solving the problem. When students make a wrong step in the process, they can retrace the step without erasing or canceling it.

The other advantage is that this strategy helps develop a better understanding of the problem or solution through visual objects or images. In this way, students will be better able to remember how to solve these types of problems.

Some of the commonly used objects for this strategy are toothpicks, straws, cards, strings, water, sand, pencils, paper, and dice.

4. Look for a Pattern

This strategy requires the use of observational and analytical skills. Students have to observe the given data to find a pattern in order to solve the problem. Math word problems that involve the use of this strategy usually have repeated numbers or patterns.

Example: Find the sum of all the numbers from 1 to 100.

Step 1: Simplify the problem.

Find the sum of 1, 2, 3, 4, 5, 6, 7, 8, 9, and 10.

Step 2: Look for a pattern.

$1 + 10 = 11$	$2 + 9 = 11$	$3 + 8 = 11$
$4 + 7 = 11$	$5 + 6 = 11$	

Step 3: Describe the pattern.

When finding the sum of 1 to 10, add the first and last numbers to get a result of 11. Then, add the second and second last numbers to get the same result. The pattern continues until all the numbers from 1 to 10 are added. There will be 5 pairs of such results. Since each addition equals 11, the answer is then $5 \times 11 = 55$.

Step 4: Use the pattern to find the answer.

Since there are 5 pairs in the sum of 1 to 10, there should be ($10 \times 5 = 50$ pairs) in the sum of 1 to 100.

Note that the addition for each pair is not equal to 11 now. The addition for each pair is now ($1 + 100 = 101$).

$$50 \times 101 = 5050$$

The sum of all the numbers from 1 to 100 is **5,050**.

5. Working Backward

The strategy of working backward applies only to a specific type of math word problem. These word problems state the end result, and students are required to find the total number. In order to solve these word problems, students have to work backward by thinking through the correct sequence of events. The strategy of working backward allows students to use their logical reasoning and sequencing to find the answers.

Example: Sarah has a piece of ribbon. She cuts the ribbon into 4 equal parts. Each part is then cut into 3 smaller equal parts. If the length of each small part is 35 cm, how long is the piece of ribbon?

$$3 \times 35 = 105 \text{ cm}$$
$$4 \times 105 = 420 \text{ cm}$$

The piece of ribbon is **420 cm**.

6. The Before-After Concept

The Before-After concept lists all the relevant data before and after an event. Students can then compare the differences and eventually solve the problems. Usually, the Before-After concept and the mathematical model go hand in hand to solve math word problems. Note that the Before-After concept can be applied only to a certain type of math word problem, which trains students to think sequentially.

Example: Kelly has 4 times as much money as Joey. After Kelly uses some money to buy a tennis racquet, and Joey uses $30 to buy a pair of pants, Kelly has twice as much money as Joey. If Joey has $98 in the beginning,
(a) how much money does Kelly have in the end?
(b) how much money does Kelly spend on the tennis racquet?

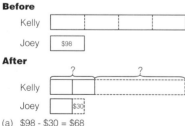

(a) $98 - $30 = $68
2 × $68 = $136
Kelly has **$136** in the end.

(b) 4 × $98 = $392
$392 – $136 = $256
Kelly spends **$256** on the tennis racquet.

7. Making Supposition

Making supposition is commonly known as "making an assumption." Students can use this strategy to solve certain types of math word problems. Making

assumptions will eliminate some possibilities and simplifies the word problems by providing a boundary of values to work within.

Example: Mrs. Jackson bought 100 pieces of candy for all the students in her class. How many pieces of candy would each student receive if there were 25 students in her class?

In the above word problem, assume that each student received the same number of pieces. This eliminates the possibilities that some students would receive more than others due to good behaviour, better results, or any other reason.

8. Representation of Problem

In problem solving, students often use representations in the solutions to show their understanding of the problems. Using representations also allow students to understand the mathematical concepts and relationships as well as to manipulate the information presented in the problems. Examples of representations are diagrams and lists or tables.

Diagrams allow students to consolidate or organize the information given in the problems. By drawing a diagram, students can see the problem clearly and solve it effectively.

A list or table can help students organize information that is useful for analysis. After analyzing, students can then see a pattern, which can be used to solve the problem.

9. Guess and Check

One of the most important and effective problem-solving techniques is Guess and Check. It is also known as Trial and Error. As the name suggests, students have to guess the answer to a problem and check if that guess is correct. If the guess is wrong, students will make another guess. This will continue until the guess is correct.

It is beneficial to keep a record of all the guesses and checks in a table. In addition, a Comments column can be included. This will enable students to analyze their guess (if it is too high or too low) and improve on the next guess. Be careful; this problem-solving technique can be tiresome without systematic or logical guesses.

Example: Jessica had 15 coins. Some of them were 10-cent coins and the rest were 5-cent coins. The total amount added up to $1.25. How many coins of each kind were there?

Use the guess-and-check method.

Number of 10¢ Coins	Value	Number of 5¢ Coins	Value	Total Number of Coins	Total Value
7	7 × 10¢ = 70¢	8	8 × 5¢ = 40¢	7 + 8 = 15	70¢ + 40¢ = 110¢ = $1.10
8	8 × 10¢ = 80¢	7	7 × 5¢ = 35¢	8 + 7 = 15	80¢ + 35¢ = 115¢ = $1.15
10	10 × 10¢ = 100¢	5	5 × 5¢ = 25¢	10 + 5 = 15	100¢ + 25¢ = 125¢ = $1.25

There were **ten** 10-cent coins and **five** 5-cent coins.

10. Restate the Problem

When solving challenging math problems, conventional methods may not be workable. Instead, restating the problem will enable students to see some challenging problems in a different light so that they can better understand them.

The strategy of restating the problem is to "say" the problem in a different and clearer way. However, students have to ensure that the main idea of the problem is not altered.

How do students restate a math problem?

First, read and understand the problem. Gather the given facts and unknowns. Note any condition(s) that have to be satisfied.

Next, restate the problem. Imagine narrating this problem to a friend. Present the given facts, unknown(s), and condition(s). Students may want to write the "revised" problem. Once the "revised" problem is analyzed, students should be able to think of an appropriate strategy to solve it.

11. Simplify the Problem

One of the commonly used strategies in mathematical problem solving is simplification of the problem. When a problem is simplified, it can be "broken down" into two or more smaller parts. Students can then solve the parts systematically to get to the final answer.

Table of Contents

Word Problems

1-70

Question 1

There are 425 apples in Basket A and 381 apples in Basket B. How many apples are there in the two baskets?

There are ⬚ apples in the two baskets.

Question 2

Michael has 55 stickers. James has 28 fewer stickers than Michael. How many stickers does James have?

James has ( ) stickers.

Question 3

Eric has 350 seashells. He has 60 seashells more than Anna-Maria. How many seashells does Anna-Maria have?

Anna-Maria has [   ] seashells.

Question 4

After lending Michiko 64 pieces of colored paper, Henry had 49 pieces left. How many pieces of colored paper did Henry have in the beginning?

Henry had ⬚ pieces of colored paper in the beginning.

Question 5

Madison completed 431 questions in her workbook. 214 of her answers were correct. How many answers were wrong?

[   ] answers were wrong.

Question 6

Ms. Jackson had some stamps. She gave 31 stamps to Kyra, 57 stamps to Darius, and had 21 stamps left. How many stamps did Ms. Jackson have in the beginning?

Ms. Jackson had ⬭ stamps in the beginning.

Question 7

Randy has 83 balloons. Kaylee has 21 fewer balloons than him. How many balloons does Kaylee have?

Kaylee has ⬭ balloons.

Question 8

Mr. Garcia sold 341 eggs on Monday. He sold 291 eggs on Tuesday. How many more eggs did he sell on Monday than on Tuesday?

He sold ⬡ more eggs on Monday than on Tuesday.

Question 9

A television set costs $581, and a DVD player costs $289. Mr. Ito paid the cashier $1,000.

(a)   How much did the television set and the DVD player cost altogether?

(b)   How much change did Mr. Ito receive from the cashier?

(a)

The television set and the DVD player cost $ ⬚.

(b)

Mr. Ito received $ ⬚ in change.

Question 10

Dad gave Tyler and Emily the same amount of pocket money. Emily bought a T-shirt for $41, and she had $6 left. How much money did Dad give Tyler?

Dad gave Tyler $ ☐ .

Question 11

After collecting 89 ice-cream sticks, Ahmad had 501 ice-cream sticks altogether. How many ice-cream sticks did he have in the beginning?

He had ⬚ ice-cream sticks in the beginning.

Question 12

Alexis has $53. She needs $29 more to buy a scooter. What is the cost of the scooter?

The cost of the scooter is $ ⬚.

Question 13

Joseph has 99 marbles. He has 35 more marbles than Elijah. How many marbles does Elijah have?

Elijah has (_____) marbles.

Alex has 281 stickers. His sister gives him another 29 stickers.
(a)   How many stickers does Alex have now?
(b)   If Alex gives 99 stickers to his friend, how many stickers does he have left?

(a)

Alex has [   ] stickers now.

(b)

He has [   ] stickers left.

Question 15

Taneesha has 345 stamps. Stephen has 56 fewer stamps than her. Lily has 9 stamps more than Taneesha.

(a)　How many stamps does Stephen have?

(b)　How many stamps does Lily have?

(a)

Stephen has ⬭ stamps.

(b)

Lily has ⬭ stamps.

Question 16

Mr. Bell baked some cookies. After selling 341 cookies, he had 39 cookies left. How many cookies did Mr. Bell bake?

Mr. Bell baked ⟮_____⟯ cookies.

Question 17

Lucy had 536 stamps. She gave 312 stamps to Salima and used 102 stamps to mail greeting cards. How many stamps did she have left?

She had ⬚ stamps left.

Question 18

There are 316 boys in Green Valley Elementary School. There are 180 more boys than girls.

(a)   How many girls are in the school?

(b)   What is the total number of students in the school?

(a)

There are ⬚ girls in the school.

(b)

The total number of students in the school is ⬚.

Question 19

A red stick is 189 cm long. A white stick is 85 cm long. How much longer is the red stick than the white stick?

The red stick is [_____] cm longer than the white stick.

Question 20

Jorge sold 350 oranges in the morning and another 81 oranges in the afternoon. He still had 65 oranges left at the end of the day. How many oranges did he have in the beginning?

He had ⬭ oranges in the beginning.

Question 21

There were 378 boys and 209 girls in the school choir last year. 95 boys and 35 girls joined the school choir this year.

(a)   How many students were in the school choir last year?

(b)   How many students joined the school choir this year?

(a)

[   ] students were in the school choir last year.

(b)

[   ] students joined the school choir this year.

Question 22

Nicholas and his brother each have 421 marbles. Nicholas receives 59 more marbles from his friend.

(a)   How many marbles does Nicholas have now?

(b)   How many marbles do Nicholas and his brother have altogether?

(a)

Nicholas has ⬭ marbles now.

(b)

Nicholas and his brother have ⬭ marbles altogether.

Question 23

Mrs. Spisak baked 250 chocolate cookies. She baked 79 fewer strawberry cookies than chocolate cookies. How many strawberry cookies did she bake?

She baked ⬭ strawberry cookies.

There are 458 girls and 641 boys in the school auditorium. How many more boys than girls are there in the auditorium?

There are ⬚ more boys than girls in the school auditorium.

Question 25

Max, Noel, Yoko, and Julia shared 36 grapes equally. How many grapes did each of them get?

Each of them got ( ) grapes.

Question 26

Mrs. Cook has 3 bags of oranges. Each bag contains 4 oranges.
(a)   How many oranges does she have altogether?
(b)   If she takes all the oranges out of the bags and puts an equal
      amount on 2 plates, how many oranges will there be on each plate?

(a)

She has [　　　　　] oranges altogether.

(b)

There will be [　　　　　] oranges on each plate.

Question 27

Jasmine had some money in her purse. She used $251 to buy a ring and had $25 left. How much money did she have in the beginning?

She had $ [   ] in the beginning.

Question 28

1 lb. of fish costs $9. What is the cost of 3 lb. of fish?

The cost of 3 lb. of fish is $ ⬚ .

Question 29

A red notebook costs twice as much as a pink notebook. If the red notebook costs $18, what is the price of the pink notebook?

The price of the pink notebook is $ [   ].

Question 30

There are 5 pencils in a bag. There are 3 times as many pens as pencils in the same bag. How many pens are in the bag?

There are ⬭ pens in the bag.

Question 31

Clara bought a dress for $16. She gave the cashier $20 and got back the change in 1-dollar bills. How many dollar bills did she get back?

She got (⬚) 1-dollar bills back.

Question 32

Each tennis racket cost $37. Each tennis ball cost $2. Luisa bought a tennis racket and 10 balls.
(a)   How much did 10 balls cost?
(b)   How much did she spend altogether?

(a)

10 balls cost $ [ ].

(b)

She spent $ [ ] altogether.

Question 33

Ella has 33 fewer greeting cards than Andy. If Andy has 101 greeting cards, how many greeting cards does Ella have?

Ella has (⬚) greeting cards.

Question 34

Liam put 128 red marbles into Bag A, 215 green marbles into Bag B, and some white marbles into Bag C. He put a total of 500 marbles into the 3 bags.
(a)   How many marbles were there altogether in Bag A and Bag B?
(b)   How many white marbles did he put into Bag C?

(a)

There were [   ] marbles altogether in Bag A and Bag B.

(b)

He put [   ] white marbles into Bag C.

Name_____

There are 250 adults, 60 girls, and 30 boys on a train. How many more adults are there than children?

There are ⬚ more adults than children.

Question 36

Uncle Sam had 3 apple trees. He picked 8 apples from each tree.
(a)   How many apples did he pick altogether?
(b)   Uncle Sam shared all the apples equally among his 4 children. How many apples did each child get?

(a)

He picked [   ] apples altogether.

(b)

Each child got [   ] apples.

Question 37

Meena, Lauren, and Minh shared 30 crackers equally among themselves.
(a)   How many crackers did each girl get?
(b)   How many crackers did Meena and Lauren have altogether?

(a)

Each girl got ⬚ crackers.

(b)

Meena and Lauren had ⬚ crackers altogether.

Name_____

Boxes A, B, and C have a total weight of 85 kg. Boxes A and B have a total weight of 46 kg.
(a)   Find the weight of Box C.
(b)   If Box C is 21 kg heavier than Box A, find the weight of Box A.

(a)

The weight of Box C is ⬚ kg.

(b)

The weight of Box A is ⬚ kg.

Question 39

Mr. Rulaski gives $30 to Bailey and Jenny. If Bailey gets twice as much money as Jenny, how much will Jenny get?

Jenny will get $ ⬚ .

Question 40

Mrs. Washington gives $20 to Isaac and Charlie. If Isaac gets 4 times as much as Charlie, how much will Charlie get?

Charlie will get $ ⬚ .

Question 41

Tierra has 7 flowers. Megan has twice as many flowers as Tierra. How many flowers do the girls have altogether?

They have ⬚ flowers altogether.

Question 42

Emilio bought a watch and a pen. The watch cost 3 times as much as the pen. If Emilio paid $5 for the pen, how much did he pay for the watch?

He paid $ ⬚ for the watch.

Question 43

Kimiko had 18 colored pencils. She shared them equally with her sister. How many colored pencils did Kimiko get?

Kimiko got ⬭ colored pencils.

Name_____

After giving $10 to each of her 4 children, Mrs. Halpert had $80 left.
(a) How much did she give to her children?
(b) How much did she have in the beginning?

(a)

She gave $ ⬚ to her children.

(b)

She had $ ⬚ in the beginning.

Name_____

Question 45

Mr. Cowen gave some apples to 6 children. He gave 1 green apple to each child. He also gave 1 red apple to every 2 children to share. How many apples did Mr. Cowen give to the children altogether?

Mr. Cowen gave the children [   ] apples altogether.

Question 46

Mrs. Rice made 37 dinner rolls. She put 5 rolls on each plate and had 2 rolls left over. How many plates did she use?

She used ⬭ plates.

Question 47

Dylan has 30 dog biscuits. He puts 5 biscuits in each box. How many boxes of dog biscuits does Dylan have?

Dylan has ⬭ boxes of dog biscuits.

Question 48

Ben gave 158 baseball cards to Antonio and 45 cards to Harry. He had 42 cards left.
(a)   How many baseball cards did Ben give away?
(b)   How many baseball cards did Ben have in the beginning?

(a)

Ben gave away [   ] baseball cards.

(b)

Ben had [   ] baseball cards in the beginning.

Question 49

Elizabeth bought 5 muffins and 5 loaves of bread for $3 each. How much did she pay in all?

She paid $ ⬚ in all.

Question 50

Hasaan had 8 marbles. His friend gave him some more marbles. Then, he had 21 marbles. How many marbles did his friend give him?

His friend gave him ⬚ marbles.

Question 51

10 children took part in the Fourth of July celebration. 6 of them were girls. If each child carried 5 flags,
(a)   how many flags did the girls carry?
(b)   how many flags did the children carry altogether?

(a)

The girls carried ⬭ flags.

(b)

The children carried ⬭ flags altogether.

Question 52

A bag of flour and 3 bags of sugar have a total weight of 21 lb. If the bag of flour weighs 6 lb., what is the weight of each bag of sugar?

The weight of each bag of sugar is [   ] lb.

Question 53

Mia has a few packets of stickers. There are 5 stickers in each packet.
(a)   How many packets of stickers does she have if she has 40 stickers in all?
(b)   If Mia shares her stickers with 3 other friends, how many stickers will each of them get?

(a)

She has ⬚ packets of stickers.

(b)

Each of them will get ⬚ stickers.

Question 54

Mr. Wood ordered 6 boxes of 10 apples each for his fruit stand. When he opened the boxes, he found 12 rotten apples.

(a)   How many apples were there altogether?

(b)   How many good apples were there?

(a)

There were ⬡ apples altogether.

(b)

There were ⬡ good apples.

Name_____

Cameron spent $800 in the first 3 months of the year. He spent $279 in February and $50 more in March than in February.

(a) How much money did he spend in March?

(b) How much money did he spend in January?

(a)

He spent $ [   ] in March.

(b)

He spent $ [   ] in January.

Question 56

Every day, Mrs. Romano mixes 22 gal. of water with 11 gal. of lemon syrup to make drinks to sell. How many gallons of drinks does she make every day?

She makes ⬭ gallons of drinks every day.

Jack's weight is 29 kg. Binh is 9 kg heavier than Jack. Cooper is 8 kg lighter than Binh.
(a)   What is Binh's weight?
(b)   What is Cooper's weight?

(a)

Binh's weight is ⬚ kg.

(b)

Cooper's weight is ⬚ kg.

Question 58

Luis had 100 oranges. 30 of them were rotten. He packed the rest equally into 10 boxes.

(a)   How many good oranges were there?

(b)   How many oranges were there in each box?

(a)

There were ⬚ good oranges.

(b)

There were ⬚ oranges in each box.

Question 59

Natasha has $10. Zoe has twice as much money as Natasha. Allison has $40 more than Zoe.

(a)   How much money does Zoe have?

(b)   How much money does Allison have?

(a)

Zoe has $ [   ].

(b)

Allison has $ [   ].

Question 60

A workbook costs 70 cents. A box of colored pencils costs 90 cents more than the workbook. How much do the workbook and the box of colored pencils cost altogether?

They cost ⌒_____⌒ cents altogether.

Question 61

Simon has 8 five-cent coins and 5 ten-cent coins.
(a)   How much money does he have in five-cent coins?
(b)   How much money does he have in ten-cent coins?

(a)

He has [   ] cents in five-cent coins.

(b)

He has [   ] cents in ten-cent coins.

Question 62

12 people took part in a race. Jonah was 7th from the front. He later overtook 3 people. How many people were behind Jonah at the end of the race?

(⬚) people were behind Jonah at the end of the race.

Question 63

Malik has 10 stamps. Kevin has 3 times as many stamps as Malik. How many stamps do they have altogether?

They have [   ] stamps altogether.

Question 64

4 teachers and 40 girls went on an overnight school trip. There were 5 girls in each room. The 4 teachers slept in 2 rooms. How many rooms did the group use altogether?

The group used ⬚ rooms altogether.

Question 65

Aaron picked 102 strawberries. He ate 13 of them and kept 39 for himself. His 5 friends shared the rest of the strawberries. How many strawberries did his friends get?

His friends got (　　　　　) strawberries.

Question 66

Gabby is twice as old as Carson. Henry is three times as old as Carson. If Henry is 30 years old, how old is Gabby?

Gabby is ⬚ years old.

Question 67

Becca gave Jeremy $30. He spent $4 each day.
(a)   How much money did he spend in a week?
(b)   How much money did he have left after a week?

(a)

He spent $ [   ] in a week.

(b)

He had $ [   ] left after a week.

Question 68

Mrs. Wylie poured 40 L of apple juice equally into 4 red jugs and 1 blue jug. How many liters of apple juice were there in each jug?

There were [   ] liters of apple juice in each jug.

Question 69

The total weight of 5 boxes of fruit is 40 lb. What is the weight of 3 boxes of fruit?

The weight of 3 boxes of fruit is ⬚ lb.

Question 70

Mackenzie picked some tomatoes from the garden. She put 4 tomatoes into each plastic bag. How many tomatoes did she pick if she used 7 plastic bags?

She picked ⬚ tomatoes.

Solutions to Word Problems 1-70

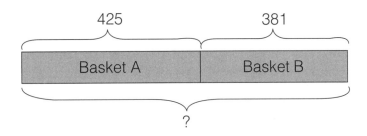

425   381

| Basket A | Basket B |

?

Use the adding-by-regrouping method.

$$425 + 381 = 806$$

$$
\begin{array}{r}
{}^{1}4\ 2\ 5 \\
+\ 3\ 8\ 1 \\
\hline
8\ 0\ 6
\end{array}
$$

There are (**806**) apples in the two baskets.

Solution to Question 2

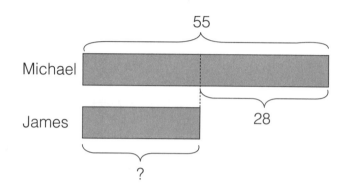

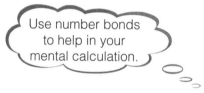

Use number bonds
to help in your
mental calculation.

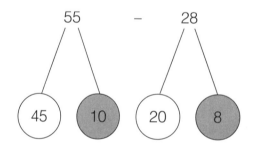

$$10 - 8 = 2$$
$$45 - 20 = 25$$
$$2 + 25 = 27$$

$$55 - 28 = 27$$

James has [**27**] stickers.

Solution to Question 3

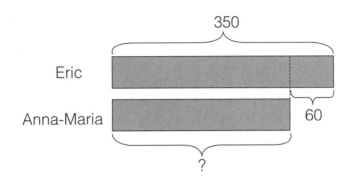

350

Eric

Anna-Maria

60

?

Use number bonds to help in your mental calculation.

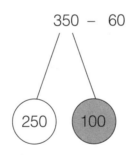

350 – 60

250   100

100 – 60 = 40
40 + 250 = 290

350 – 60 = 290

Anna-Maria has ⟨ **290** ⟩ seashells.

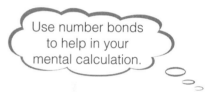

Use number bonds to help in your mental calculation.

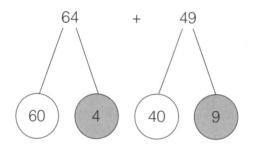

$$4 + 9 = 13$$
$$60 + 40 = 100$$
$$13 + 100 = 113$$

$$64 + 49 = 113$$

Henry had ⌈ **113** ⌉ pieces of colored paper in the beginning.

Solution to Question 5

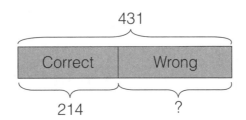

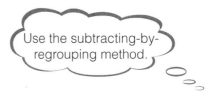

Use the subtracting-by-regrouping method.

$$431 - 214 = 217$$

$$\begin{array}{r} 4\ \overset{2}{\cancel{3}}\ \overset{11}{\cancel{1}} \\ -\ 2\ 1\ 4 \\ \hline 2\ 1\ 7 \end{array}$$

217 answers were wrong.

Solution to Question 6

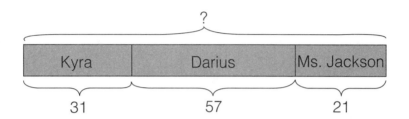

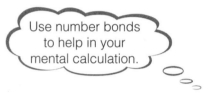

Use number bonds to help in your mental calculation.

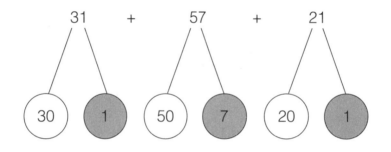

$$1 + 7 + 1 = 9$$
$$30 + 50 + 20 = 100$$
$$9 + 100 = 109$$

$$31 + 57 + 21 = 109$$

Ms. Jackson had 109 stamps in the beginning.

Solution to Question 7

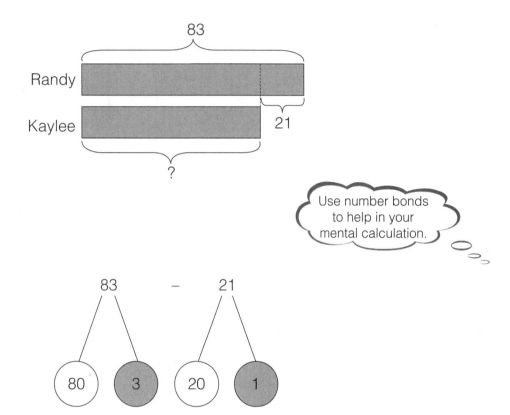

83

Randy

Kaylee

21

?

Use number bonds to help in your mental calculation.

83 − 21

80   3   20   1

$3 - 1 = 2$
$80 - 20 = 60$
$2 + 60 = 62$

$83 - 21 = 62$

Kaylee has   **62**   balloons.

Solution to Question 8

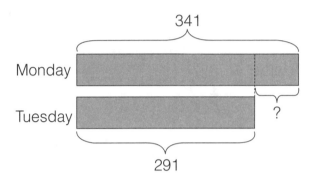

341

Monday

Tuesday

?

291

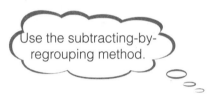

Use the subtracting-by-regrouping method.

$$341 - 291 = 50$$

```
      2  14
   3  4  1
 - 2  9  1
 ─────────
      5  0
```

He sold (50) more eggs on Monday than on Tuesday.

Solution to Question 9

(a)

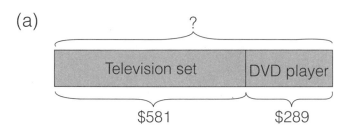

$581 + $289 = $870

> Use the adding-by-regrouping-twice method.

$$\begin{array}{r} \overset{1}{5}\,\overset{1}{8}\,1 \\ +\ 2\,8\,9 \\ \hline 8\,7\,0 \end{array}$$

The television set and the DVD player cost $ [**870**].

(b)

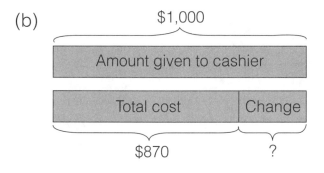

> Use number bonds to help in your mental calculation.

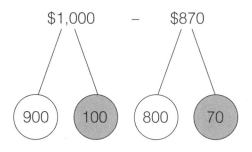

$100 - 70 = 30$
$900 - 800 = 100$
$30 + 100 = 130$

$1,000 - $870 = $130

Mr. Ito received $ [**130**] in change.

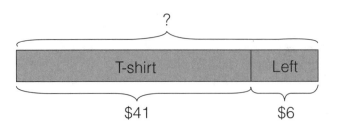

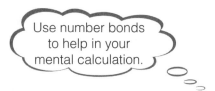

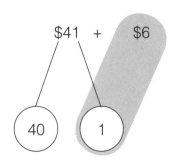

$$1 + 6 = 7$$
$$7 + 40 = 47$$

$$\$41 + \$6 = \$47$$

Dad gave Tyler $ [**47**].

Solution to Question 11

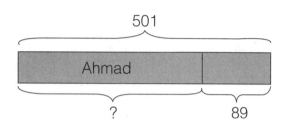

501

Ahmad

? 89

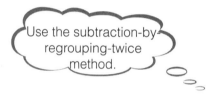

Use the subtraction-by-regrouping-twice method.

$$501 - 89 = 412$$

$$
\begin{array}{r}
{\scriptstyle 4\ \ 9\ \ 11} \\
\not5\ \not0\ \not1 \\
-\ \ 8\ 9 \\
\hline
4\ 1\ 2
\end{array}
$$

He had 　412　 ice-cream sticks in the beginning.

Solution to Question 12

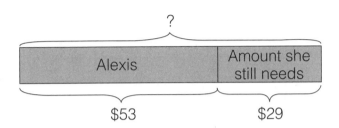

?

Alexis	Amount she still needs

$53 $29

Use number bonds to help in your mental calculation.

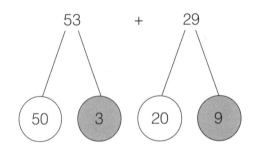

53   +   29

50   3   20   9

3 + 9 = 12
50 + 20 = 70
12 + 70 = 82

$53 + $29 = $82

The cost of the scooter is $ [**82**].

Solution to Question 13

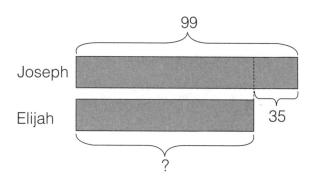

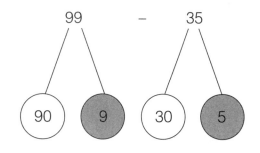

Use number bonds to help in your mental calculation.

$$9 - 5 = 4$$
$$90 - 30 = 60$$
$$4 + 60 = 64$$

$$99 - 35 = 64$$

Elijah has ⟨ **64** ⟩ marbles.

(a)

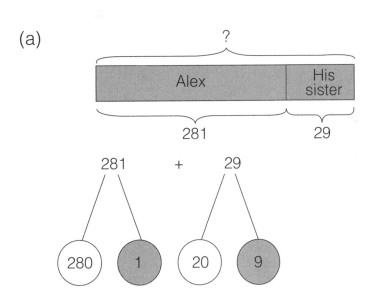

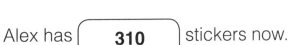

$1 + 9 = 10$
$280 + 20 = 300$
$10 + 300 = 310$

$281 + 29 = 310$

Alex has [**310**] stickers now.

(b)

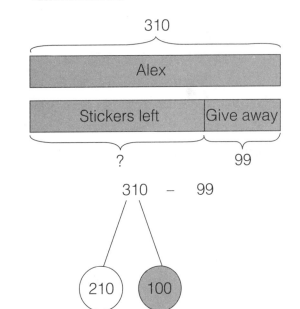

$100 - 99 = 1$
$1 + 210 = 211$

$310 - 99 = 211$

He has [**211**] stickers left.

Solution to Question 15

(a)

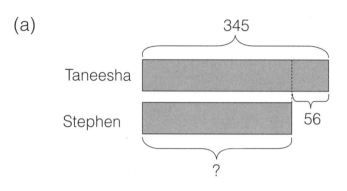

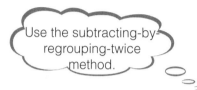

Use the subtracting-by-regrouping-twice method.

$$345 - 56 = 289$$

$$\begin{array}{r} \overset{2}{\cancel{3}}\ \overset{13}{\cancel{4}}\ \overset{15}{\cancel{5}} \\ -\ \ \ 5\ 6 \\ \hline 2\ 8\ 9 \end{array}$$

Stephen has **289** stamps.

(b)

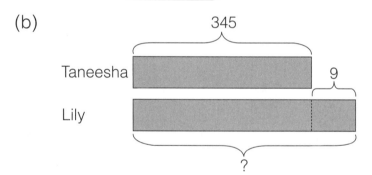

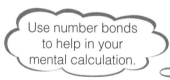

Use number bonds to help in your mental calculation.

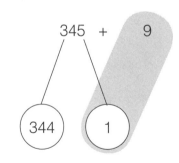

$$1 + 9 = 10$$
$$10 + 344 = 354$$
$$345 + 9 = 354$$

Lily has **354** stamps.

Solution to Question 16

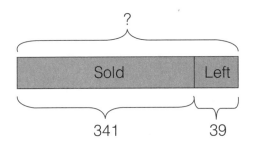

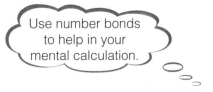

Use number bonds to help in your mental calculation.

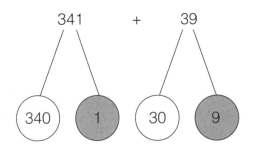

$$1 + 9 = 10$$
$$340 + 30 = 370$$
$$10 + 370 = 380$$

$$341 + 39 = 380$$

Mr. Bell baked ⎡ **380** ⎤ cookies.

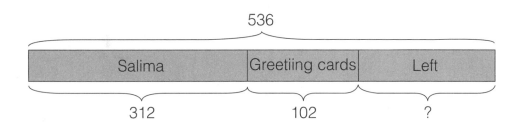

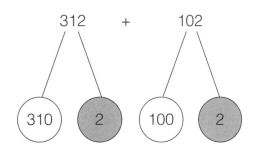

Use number bonds to help in your mental calculation.

$$2 + 2 = 4$$
$$310 + 100 = 410$$
$$4 + 410 = 414$$

$$312 + 102 = 414$$

Use the subtracting-without-regrouping method.

$$536 - 414 = 122$$

```
   5 3 6
 - 4 1 4
   1 2 2
```

She had [**122**] stamps left.

(a)

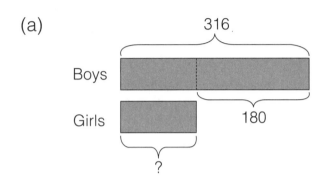

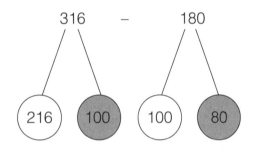

Use number bonds to help in your mental calculation.

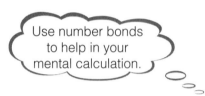

$100 - 80 = 20$
$216 - 100 = 116$
$20 + 116 = 136$

$316 - 180 = 136$

There are ⬚ 136 ⬚ girls in the school.

(b)

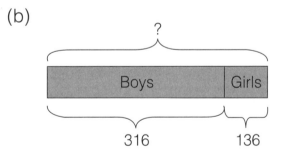

$316 + 136 = 452$

Use the adding-by-regrouping method.

$$\begin{array}{r} 3\,{}^{1}1\,6 \\ +\ 1\ 3\ 6 \\ \hline 4\ 5\ 2 \end{array}$$

The total number of students in the school is ⬚ 452 ⬚.

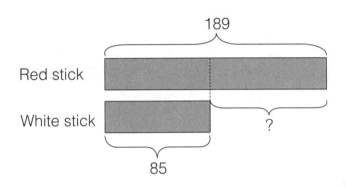

Red stick

White stick

189

85

?

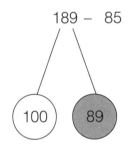

Use number bonds to help in your mental calculation.

189 – 85

100   89

89 – 85 = 4
4 + 100 = 104

189 – 85 = 104

The red stick is [**104**] cm longer than the white stick.

Solution to Question 20

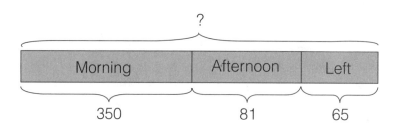

Morning	Afternoon	Left
350	81	65

Use the adding-by-regrouping method.

350 + 81 = 431

$$\begin{array}{r} {}^{1}3\ 5\ 0 \\ +\ \ 8\ 1 \\ \hline 4\ 3\ 1 \end{array}$$

Use the adding-without-regrouping method.

431 + 65 = 496

$$\begin{array}{r} 4\ 3\ 1 \\ +\ \ 6\ 5 \\ \hline 4\ 9\ 6 \end{array}$$

He had **496** oranges in the beginning.

Solution to Question 21

(a)

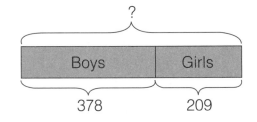

Use the adding-by-regrouping method.

$$378 + 209 = 587$$

$$\begin{array}{r} \overset{1}{3}\ 7\ 8 \\ +\ 2\ 0\ 9 \\ \hline 5\ 8\ 7 \end{array}$$

587 students were in the school choir last year.

(b)

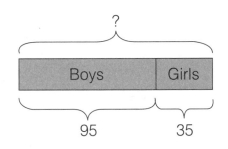

Use number bonds to help in your mental calculation.

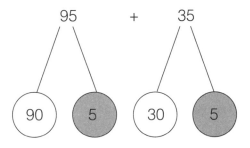

$$5 + 5 = 10$$
$$90 + 30 = 120$$
$$10 + 120 = 130$$

$$95 + 35 = 130$$

130 students joined the school choir this year.

(a)

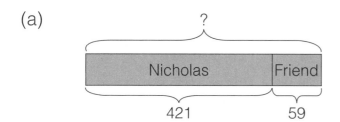

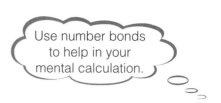

Use number bonds to help in your mental calculation.

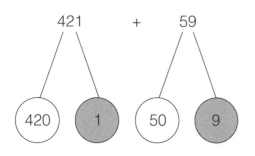

$$1 + 9 = 10$$
$$420 + 50 = 470$$
$$10 + 470 = 480$$

$$421 + 59 = 480$$

Nicholas has $\boxed{480}$ marbles now.

(b)

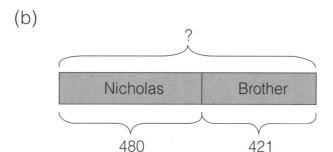

Use the adding-by-regrouping method.

$$480 + 421 = 901$$

$$\begin{array}{r} {}^{1} \\ 4\ 8\ 0 \\ +\ 4\ 2\ 1 \\ \hline 9\ 0\ 1 \end{array}$$

Nicholas and his brother have $\boxed{901}$ marbles altogether.

Solution to Question 23

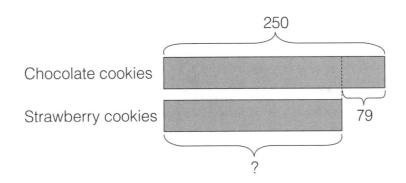

Chocolate cookies

Strawberry cookies

250

79

?

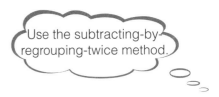

Use the subtracting-by-regrouping-twice method.

$$250 - 79 = 171$$

$$
\begin{array}{r}
\overset{1}{\cancel{2}}\,\overset{14}{\cancel{5}}\,\overset{10}{\cancel{0}} \\
-\quad 7\ 9 \\
\hline
1\ 7\ 1
\end{array}
$$

She baked (**171**) strawberry cookies.

Solution to Question 24

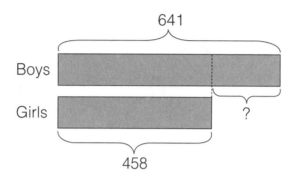

641

Boys

Girls

?

458

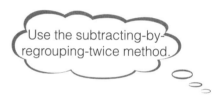
Use the subtracting-by-regrouping-twice method.

$$641 - 458 = 183$$

$$\begin{array}{r} \overset{5}{\cancel{6}}\,\overset{13}{\cancel{4}}\,\overset{11}{\cancel{1}} \\ -\ 4\ 5\ 8 \\ \hline 1\ 8\ 3 \end{array}$$

There are $\boxed{183}$ more boys than girls in the school auditorium.

Solution to Question 25

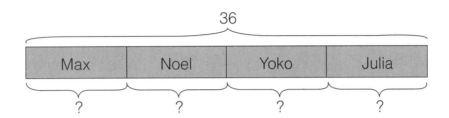

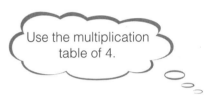

$$36 \div 4 = 9$$

Each of them got [**9**] grapes.

(a)

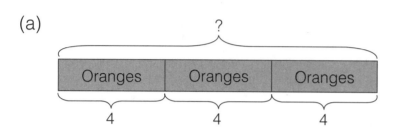

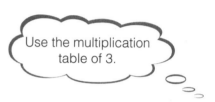

Use the multiplication table of 3.

$$3 \times 4 = 12$$

$3 \times 1 = 3$
$3 \times 2 = 6$
$3 \times 3 = 9$
$3 \times 4 = 12$

She has $\boxed{12}$ oranges altogether.

(b)

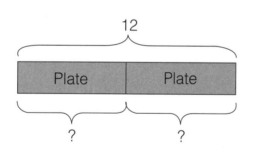

$$12 \div 2 = 6$$

Use the multiplication table of 2.

$2 \times 6 = 12$

There will be $\boxed{6}$ oranges on each plate.

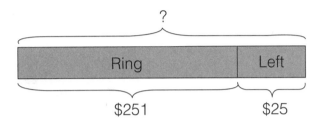

Use number bonds to help in your mental calculation.

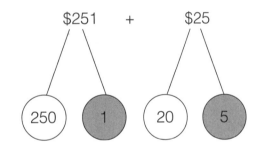

1 + 5 = 6
250 + 20 = 270
6 + 270 = 276

$251 + $25 = $276

She had $ [276] in the beginning.

Solution to Question 28

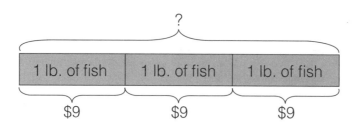

Use the multiplication table of 3.

$$3 \times \$9 = \$27$$

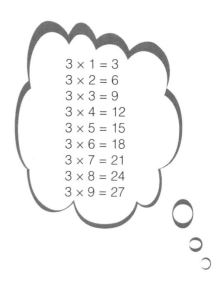

3 × 1 = 3
3 × 2 = 6
3 × 3 = 9
3 × 4 = 12
3 × 5 = 15
3 × 6 = 18
3 × 7 = 21
3 × 8 = 24
3 × 9 = 27

The cost of 3 lb. of fish is $ [**27**].

The word *twice* in the question refers to "two times." Because the red notebook is twice as much as the pink notebook, we can say that the red notebook has 2 parts, and the pink notebook has 1 part.

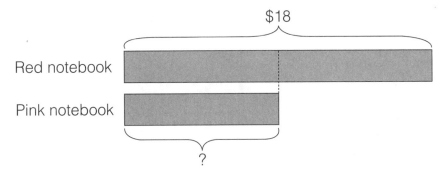

Use the multiplication table of 2.

$$\$18 \div 2 = \$9$$

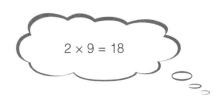

$2 \times 9 = 18$

The price of the pink notebook is $ [9].

Because there are 3 times as many pens as pencils, the pens have 3 parts and the pencils have 1 part.

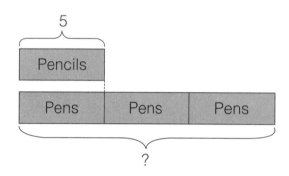

Use the multiplication table of 3.

$3 \times 5 = 15$

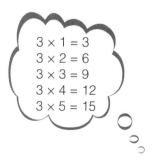

$3 \times 1 = 3$
$3 \times 2 = 6$
$3 \times 3 = 9$
$3 \times 4 = 12$
$3 \times 5 = 15$

There are 15 pens in the bag.

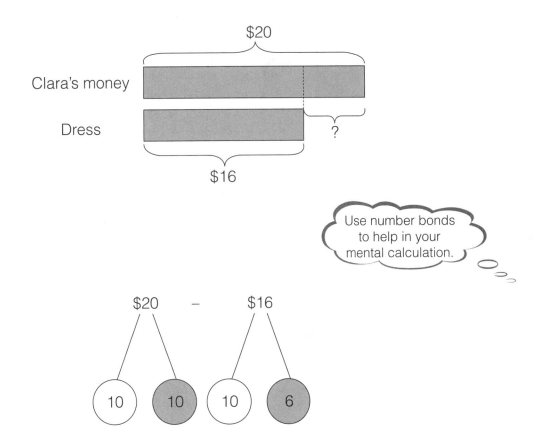

$10 - 6 = 4$
$10 - 10 = 0$
$4 + 0 = 4$

$20 - 16 = 4$

She got [4] 1-dollar bills back.

Solution to Question 32

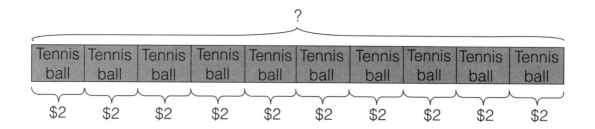

?

Tennis ball	Tennis ball	Tennis ball	Tennis ball	Tennis ball	Tennis ball	Tennis ball	Tennis ball	Tennis ball	Tennis ball
$2	$2	$2	$2	$2	$2	$2	$2	$2	$2

(a)

$$10 \times \$2 = \$20$$

10 balls cost $ [**20**].

Use the multiplication table of 2.

(b)

?

Tennis racket	Balls
$37	$20

$37 + $20

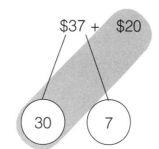
30   7

$$30 + 20 = 50$$
$$50 + 7 = 57$$

$2 × 1 = 2
2 × 2 = 4
2 × 3 = 6
2 × 4 = 8
2 × 5 = 10
2 × 6 = 12
2 × 7 = 14
2 × 8 = 16
2 × 9 = 18
2 × 10 = 20

$$\$37 + \$20 = \$57$$

Use number bonds to help in your mental calculation.

She spent $ [**57**] altogether.

Solution to Question 33

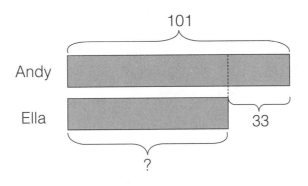

Use number bonds to help in your mental calculation.

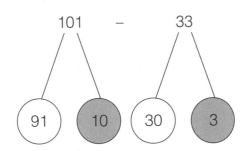

$$10 - 3 = 7$$
$$91 - 30 = 61$$
$$7 + 61 = 68$$

$$101 - 33 = 68$$

Ella has [**68**] greeting cards.

Solution to Question 34

(a)

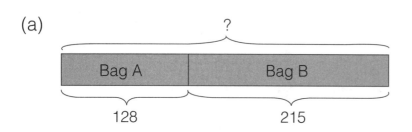

$$128 + 215 = 343$$

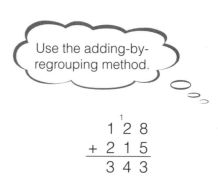

Use the adding-by-regrouping method.

$$\begin{array}{r} 1\overset{1}{2}8 \\ + 2\ 1\ 5 \\ \hline 3\ 4\ 3 \end{array}$$

There were [**343**] marbles altogether in Bag A and Bag B.

(b)

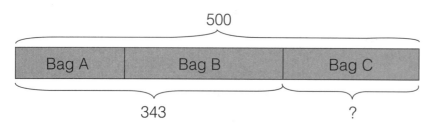

$$500 - 343 = 157$$

Use the subtracting-by-regrouping-twice method.

$$\begin{array}{r} \overset{4}{5}\overset{9}{\cancel{0}}\overset{10}{\cancel{0}} \\ -\ 3\ 4\ 3 \\ \hline 1\ 5\ 7 \end{array}$$

He put [**157**] white marbles into Bag C.

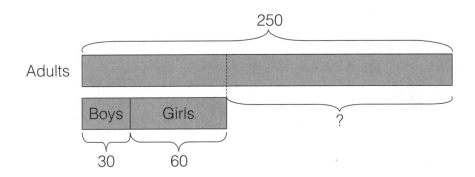

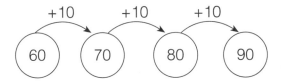

Use the counting-on method.

$$60 + 30 = 90$$

The total number of children is 90.

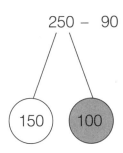

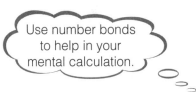

Use number bonds to help in your mental calculation.

$$100 - 90 = 10$$
$$10 + 150 = 160$$

$$250 - 90 = 160$$

There are 　160　 more adults than children.

(a)

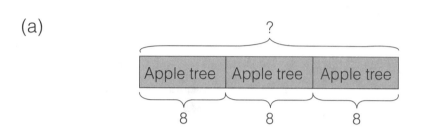

$$3 \times 8 = 24$$

Use the multiplication table of 3.

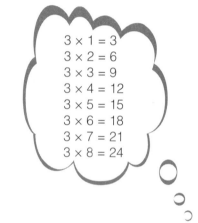

3 × 1 = 3
3 × 2 = 6
3 × 3 = 9
3 × 4 = 12
3 × 5 = 15
3 × 6 = 18
3 × 7 = 21
3 × 8 = 24

He picked ⎡ **24** ⎤ apples altogether.

(b)

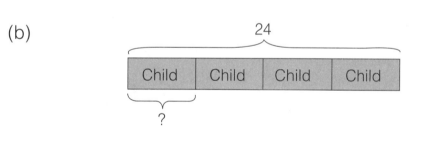

$$24 \div 4 = 6$$

Use the multiplication table of 4.

4 × 6 = 24

Each child got ⎡ **6** ⎤ apples.

Solution to Question 37

(a)

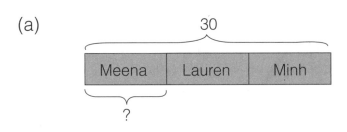

$$30 \div 3 = 10$$

Each girl got **10** crackers.

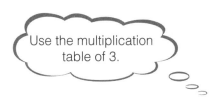

Use the multiplication table of 3.

$3 \times 10 = 30$

(b)

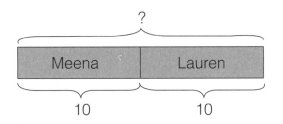

$$2 \times 10 = 20$$

Use the multiplication table of 2.

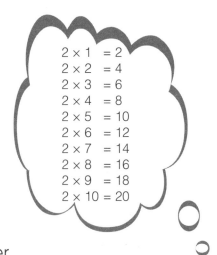

$2 \times 1 = 2$
$2 \times 2 = 4$
$2 \times 3 = 6$
$2 \times 4 = 8$
$2 \times 5 = 10$
$2 \times 6 = 12$
$2 \times 7 = 14$
$2 \times 8 = 16$
$2 \times 9 = 18$
$2 \times 10 = 20$

Meena and Lauren had **20** crackers altogether.

Solution to Question 38

(a)

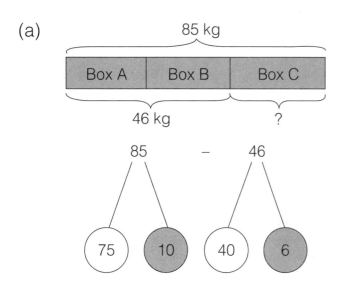

Use number bonds to help in your mental calculation.

$$10 - 6 = 4$$
$$75 - 40 = 35$$
$$4 + 35 = 39$$

$$85 - 46 = 39$$

The weight of Box C is [**39**] kg.

(b)

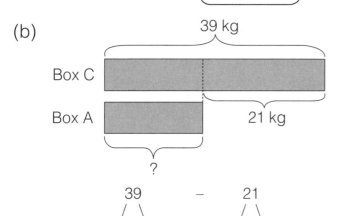

Use number bonds.

$$9 - 1 = 8$$
$$30 - 20 = 10$$
$$8 + 10 = 18$$

$$39 - 21 = 18$$

The weight of Box A is [**18**] kg.

70 Must-Know Word Problems Level 2

The word *twice* in the question refers to "two times." Because Bailey gets twice as much money as Jenny, Bailey gets 2 parts and Jenny gets 1 part.

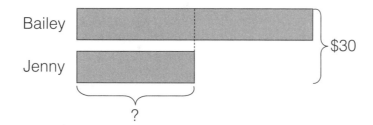

Use the multiplication table of 3.

$$\$30 \div 3 = \$10$$

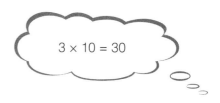

3 × 10 = 30

Jenny will get $ 　10　 .

Because Isaac gets 4 times as much as Charlie, Isaac gets 4 parts and Charlie gets 1 part.

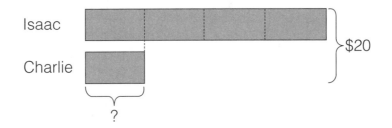

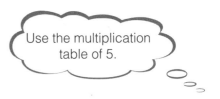

Use the multiplication table of 5.

$$\$20 \div 5 = \$4$$

$$5 \times 4 = 20$$

Charlie will get $ [4].

The word *twice* refers to "two times." Because Megan has twice as many flowers as Tierra, Megan has 2 parts and Tierra has 1 part.

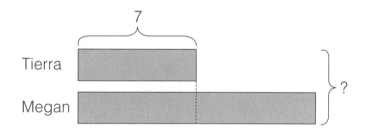

Use the multiplication table of 3.

$$3 \times 7 = 21$$

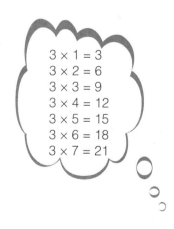

3 × 1 = 3
3 × 2 = 6
3 × 3 = 9
3 × 4 = 12
3 × 5 = 15
3 × 6 = 18
3 × 7 = 21

They have [**21**] flowers altogether.

Solution to Question 42

Because the watch cost 3 times as much as the pen, the watch has 3 parts and the pen has 1 part.

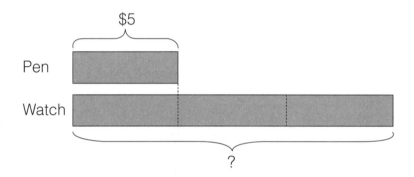

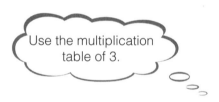

Use the multiplication table of 3.

$$3 \times \$5 = \$15$$

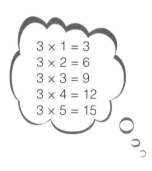

$3 \times 1 = 3$
$3 \times 2 = 6$
$3 \times 3 = 9$
$3 \times 4 = 12$
$3 \times 5 = 15$

He paid $ [**15**] for the watch.

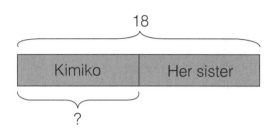

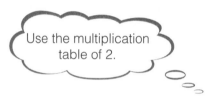

Use the multiplication table of 2.

$$18 \div 2 = 9$$

$2 \times 9 = 18$

Kimiko got [**9**] colored pencils.

(a)

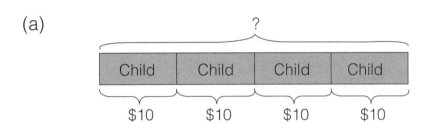

$4 \times \$10 = \$40$

She gave $\boxed{40}$ to her children.

(b)

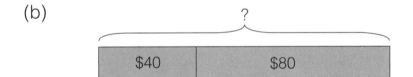

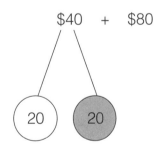

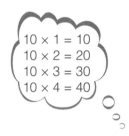

$80 + 20 = 100$
$100 + 20 = 120$

$\$40 + \$80 = \$120$

She had $\boxed{120}$ in the beginning.

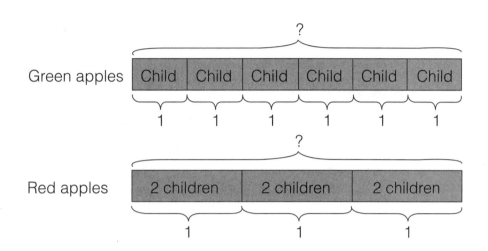

Green apples | Child | Child | Child | Child | Child | Child
1   1   1   1   1   1

Red apples | 2 children | 2 children | 2 children
1   1   1

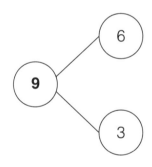

Use number bonds to help in your mental calculation.

6 + 3 = 9

Mr. Cowen gave the children [**9**] apples altogether.

Solution to Question 46

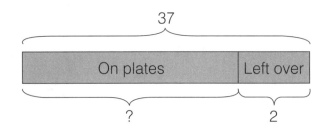

$$37 - 2 = 35$$

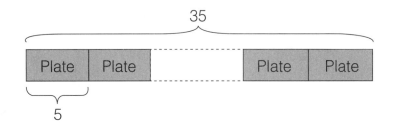

Use the multiplication table of 5.

$$35 \div 5 = 7$$

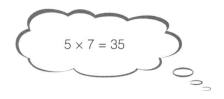

$$5 \times 7 = 35$$

She used [7] plates.

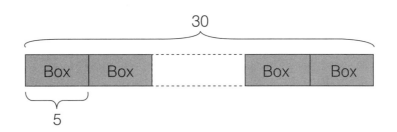

Use the multiplication table of 5.

$$30 \div 5 = 6$$

$5 \times 6 = 30$

Dylan has [**6**] boxes of dog biscuits.

Solution to Question 48

(a)

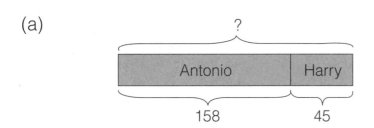

$$158 + 45 = 203$$

Ben gave away $\boxed{203}$ baseball cards.

> Use the adding-by-regrouping-twice method.

$$\begin{array}{r} {}^{1}\ {}^{1}\ \\ 1\ 5\ 8 \\ +\ \ \ 4\ 5 \\ \hline 2\ 0\ 3 \end{array}$$

(b)

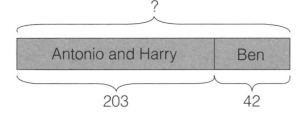

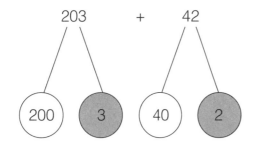

> Use number bonds to help in your mental calculation.

$$3 + 2 = 5$$
$$200 + 40 = 240$$
$$5 + 240 = 245$$

$$203 + 42 = 245$$

Ben had $\boxed{245}$ baseball cards in the beginning.

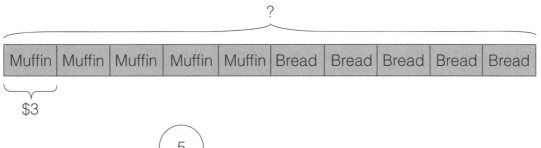

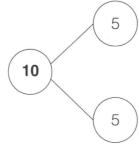

Use number bonds.

$$5 + 5 = 10$$

Use the multiplication table of 3.

$$10 \times \$3 = \$30$$

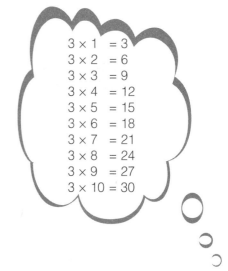
$3 \times 1 = 3$
$3 \times 2 = 6$
$3 \times 3 = 9$
$3 \times 4 = 12$
$3 \times 5 = 15$
$3 \times 6 = 18$
$3 \times 7 = 21$
$3 \times 8 = 24$
$3 \times 9 = 27$
$3 \times 10 = 30$

She paid $ [**30**] in all.

Solution to Question 50

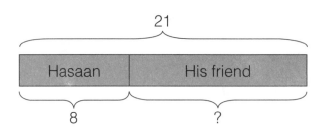

Use number bonds to help in your mental calculation.

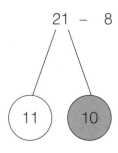

21 − 8

$10 - 8 = 2$
$2 + 11 = 13$

$21 - 8 = 13$

His friend gave him ⟨ **13** ⟩ marbles.

(a)

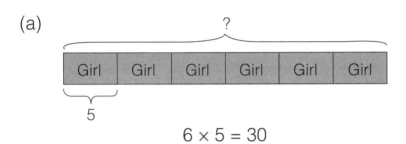

$$6 \times 5 = 30$$

The girls carried **30** flags.

> Use the multiplication table of 5.

(b)

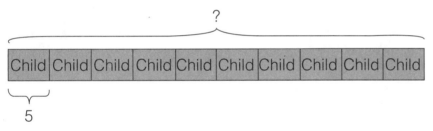

$$10 \times 5 = 50$$

$5 \times 1 = 5$
$5 \times 2 = 10$
$5 \times 3 = 15$
$3 \times 4 = 20$
$5 \times 5 = 25$
$5 \times 6 = 30$
$5 \times 7 = 35$
$5 \times 8 = 40$
$5 \times 9 = 45$
$5 \times 10 = 50$

The children carried **50** flags altogether.

Solution to Question 52

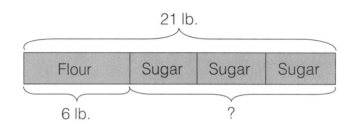

21 lb.

| Flour | Sugar | Sugar | Sugar |

6 lb.   ?

Use number bonds to help in your mental calculation.

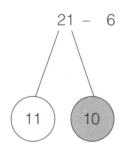

21 − 6

11   10

$10 - 6 = 4$
$4 + 11 = 15$

$21 - 6 = 15$

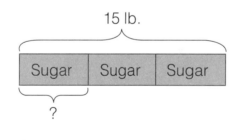

15 lb.

| Sugar | Sugar | Sugar |

?

Use the multiplication table of 3.

$15 \div 3 = 5$

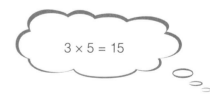

$3 \times 5 = 15$

The weight of each bag of sugar is ⟨ **5** ⟩ lb.

(a)

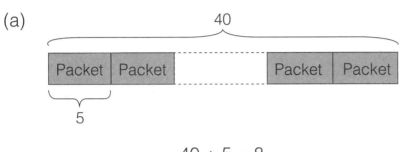

$$40 \div 5 = 8$$

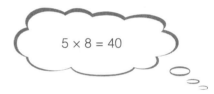

Use the multiplication table of 5.

$5 \times 8 = 40$

She has [**8**] packets of stickers.

(b)

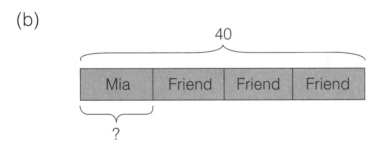

$$40 \div 4 = 10$$

Use the multiplication table of 4.

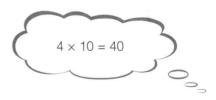

$4 \times 10 = 40$

Each of them will get [**10**] stickers.

Solution to Question 54

(a)

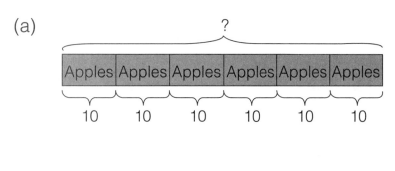

$$6 \times 10 = 60$$

There were | **60** | apples altogether.

(b)

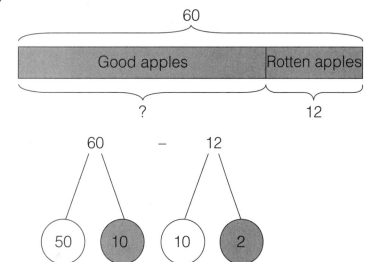

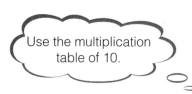

Use the multiplication table of 10.

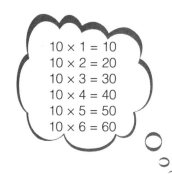

$10 \times 1 = 10$
$10 \times 2 = 20$
$10 \times 3 = 30$
$10 \times 4 = 40$
$10 \times 5 = 50$
$10 \times 6 = 60$

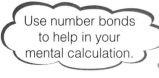

Use number bonds to help in your mental calculation.

$$10 - 2 = 8$$
$$50 - 10 = 40$$
$$8 + 40 = 48$$

$$60 - 12 = 48$$

There were | **48** | good apples.

(a)

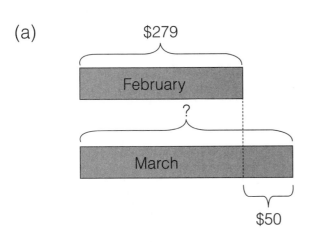

$279 + $50 = $329

He spent $ [**329**] in March.

Use the adding-by-regrouping method.

```
    1
  2 7 9
+   5 0
  3 2 9
```

(b)

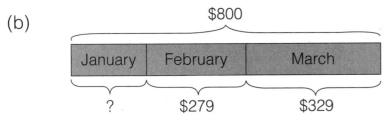

$279 + $329 = $608

```
  1 1
  2 7 9
+ 3 2 9
  6 0 8
```

Use the adding-by-regrouping-twice method.

$800 − $608 = $192

```
  7 9 10
  8 0 0
− 6 0 8
  1 9 2
```

Use the subtracting-by-regrouping-twice method.

He spent $ [**192**] in January.

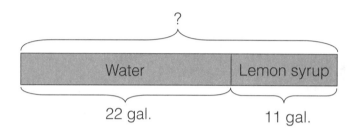

Use number bonds to help in your mental calculation.

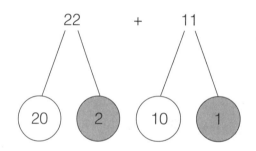

$$2 + 1 = 3$$
$$20 + 10 = 30$$
$$3 + 30 = 33$$

$$22 + 11 = 33$$

She makes [**33**] gallons of drinks every day.

(a)

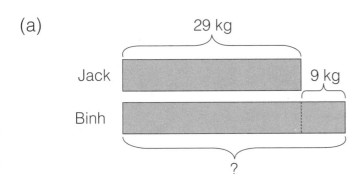

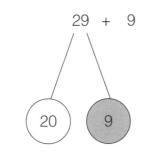

Use number bonds to help in your mental calculation.

$9 + 9 = 18$
$18 + 20 = 38$

$29 + 9 = 38$

Binh's weight is [**38**] kg.

(b)

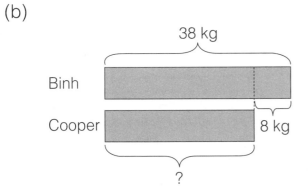

$38 - 8 = 30$

Cooper's weight is [**30**] kg.

(a)

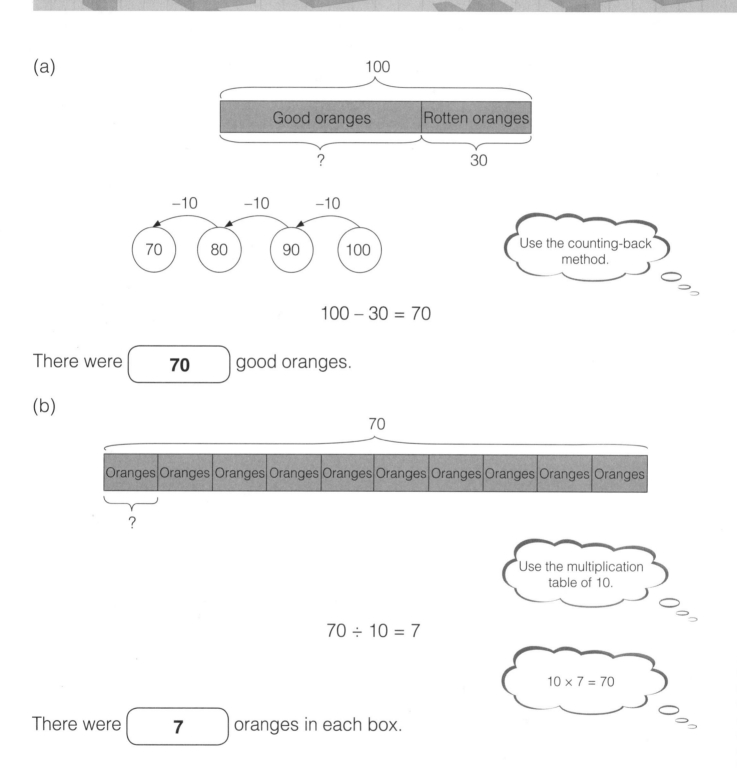

$100 - 30 = 70$

There were [**70**] good oranges.

(b)

$70 \div 10 = 7$

There were [**7**] oranges in each box.

(a) The word *twice* refers to "two times." Using the mathematical model, Natasha has 1 part and Zoe has 2 parts.

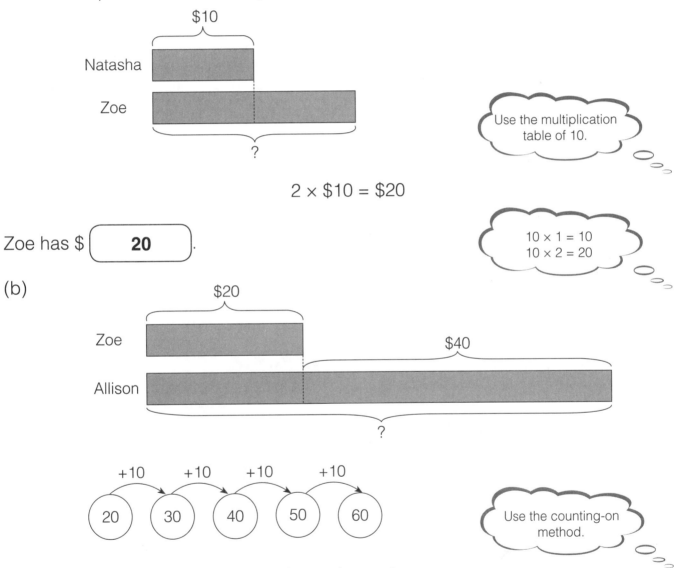

$2 \times \$10 = \$20$

Use the multiplication table of 10.

Zoe has $ [**20**].

$10 \times 1 = 10$
$10 \times 2 = 20$

(b)

$20 + 40 = 60$

$\$20 + \$40 = \$60$

Use the counting-on method.

Allison has $ [**60**].

Solution to Question 60

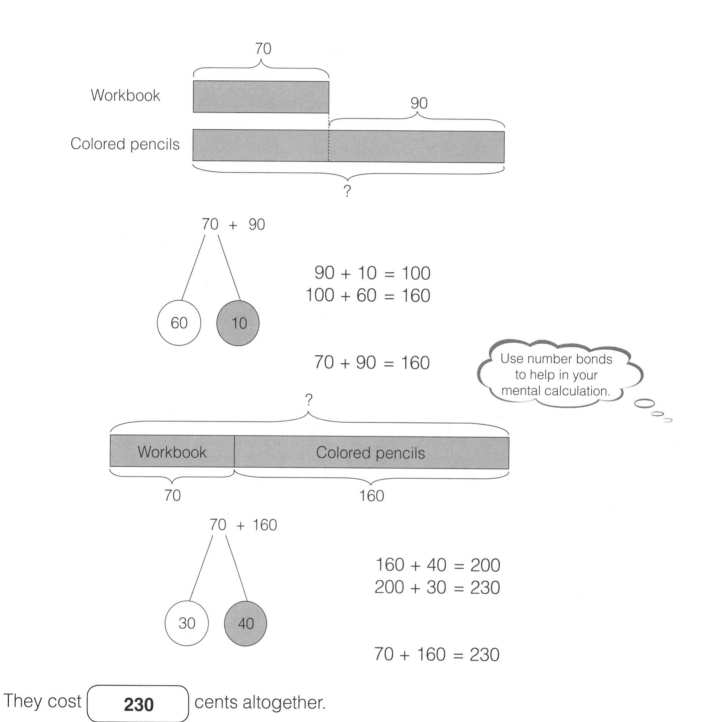

70

Workbook

90

Colored pencils

?

$70 + 90$

$$90 + 10 = 100$$
$$100 + 60 = 160$$

60   10

$$70 + 90 = 160$$

Use number bonds to help in your mental calculation.

?

| Workbook | Colored pencils |

70   160

$70 + 160$

$$160 + 40 = 200$$
$$200 + 30 = 230$$

30   40

$$70 + 160 = 230$$

They cost **230** cents altogether.

Solution to Question 61

(a)

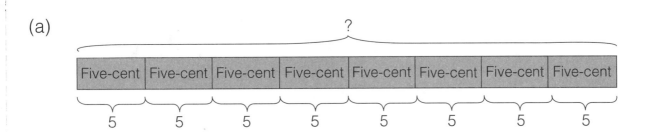

$$8 \times 5 = 40$$

Use the multiplication table of 5.

$5 \times 1 = 5$
$5 \times 2 = 10$
$5 \times 3 = 15$
$5 \times 4 = 20$
$5 \times 5 = 25$
$5 \times 6 = 30$
$5 \times 7 = 35$
$5 \times 8 = 40$

He has **40** cents in five-cent coins.

(b)

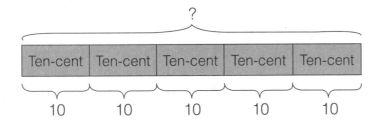

$$5 \times 10 = 50$$

Use the multiplication table of 10.

$10 \times 1 = 10$
$10 \times 2 = 20$
$10 \times 3 = 30$
$10 \times 4 = 40$
$10 \times 5 = 50$

He has **50** cents in ten-cent coins.

Solution to Question 62

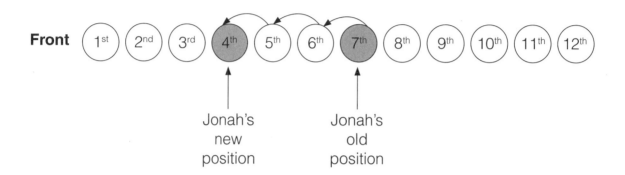

Front 1st 2nd 3rd **4th** 5th 6th **7th** 8th 9th 10th 11th 12th

Jonah's new position

Jonah's old position

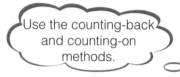

Use the counting-back and counting-on methods.

$$12 - 4 = 8$$

8 people were behind Jonah at the end of the race.

Kevin has 3 parts and Malik has 1 part.

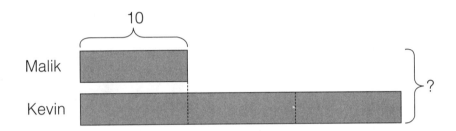

Use the multiplication table of 10.

$$10 \times 4 = 40$$

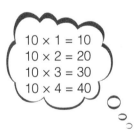

$10 \times 1 = 10$
$10 \times 2 = 20$
$10 \times 3 = 30$
$10 \times 4 = 40$

They have [**40**] stamps altogether.

Solution to Question 64

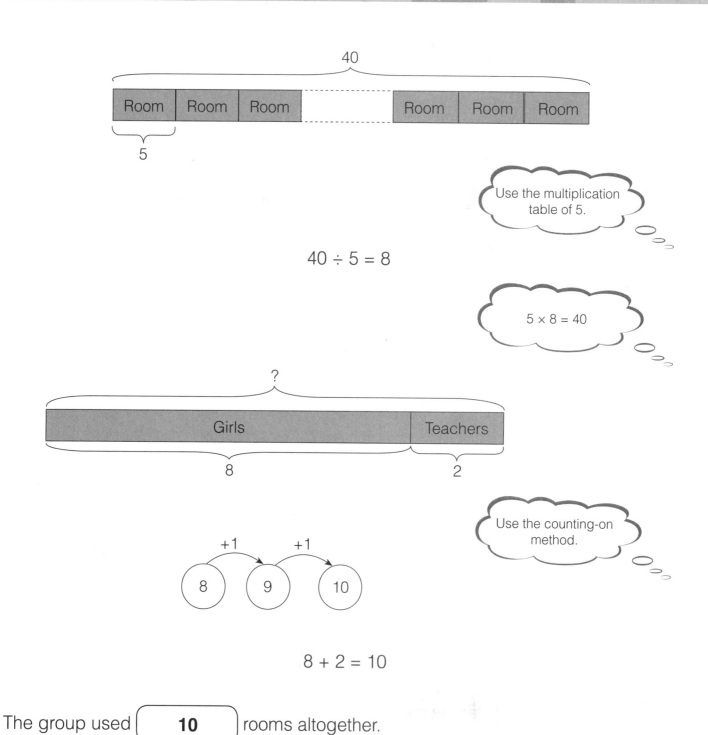

40

| Room | Room | Room | | Room | Room | Room |

5

Use the multiplication table of 5.

$$40 \div 5 = 8$$

$$5 \times 8 = 40$$

?

| Girls | Teachers |

8   2

Use the counting-on method.

+1   +1

8   →   9   →   10

$$8 + 2 = 10$$

The group used **10** rooms altogether.

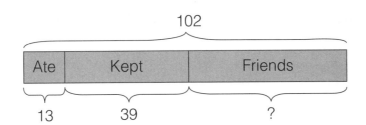

102

Ate	Kept	Friends

13   39   ?

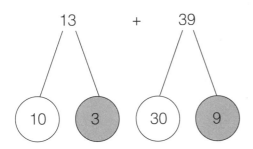

13   +   39

$3 + 9 = 12$
$10 + 30 = 40$
$12 + 40 = 52$

$13 + 39 = 52$

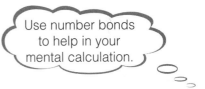

Use number bonds to help in your mental calculation.

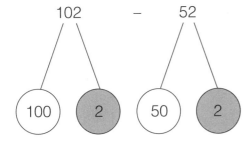

102   –   52

$2 - 2 = 0$
$100 - 50 = 50$
$0 + 50 = 50$

$102 - 52 = 50$

His friends got [**50**] strawberries.

Carson has 1 part, Gabby has 2 parts, and Henry has 3 parts.

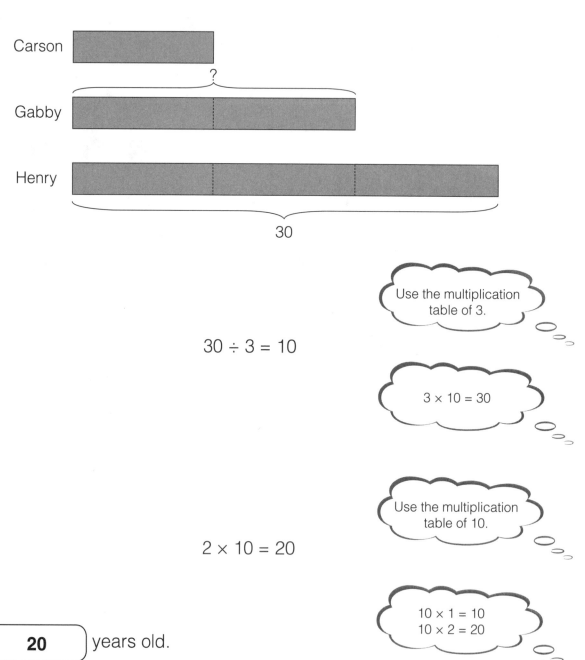

$$30 \div 3 = 10$$

Use the multiplication table of 3.

$$3 \times 10 = 30$$

$$2 \times 10 = 20$$

Use the multiplication table of 10.

$$10 \times 1 = 10$$
$$10 \times 2 = 20$$

Gabby is [**20**] years old.

(a)

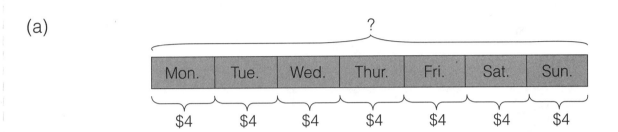

Use the multiplication table of 4.

$7 \times \$4 = \$28$

$4 \times 1 = 4$
$4 \times 2 = 8$
$4 \times 3 = 12$
$4 \times 4 = 16$
$4 \times 5 = 20$
$4 \times 6 = 24$
$4 \times 7 = 28$

He spent $ [**28**] in a week.

(b)

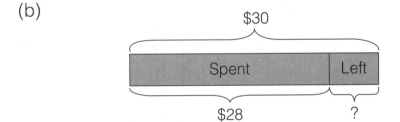

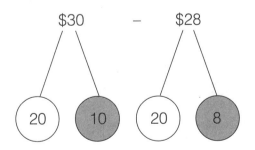

Use number bonds to help in your mental calculation.

$10 - 8 = 2$
$20 - 20 = 0$
$2 + 0 = 2$

$\$30 - \$28 = \$2$

He had $ [**2**] left after a week.

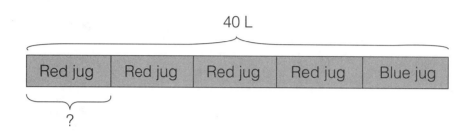

40 L

| Red jug | Red jug | Red jug | Red jug | Blue jug |

?

Use the multiplication table of 5.

$40 \div 5 = 8$

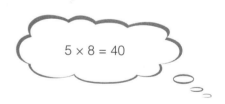

$5 \times 8 = 40$

There were ⟨ 8 ⟩ liters of apple juice in each jug.

(a)

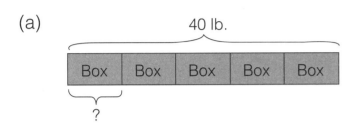

Use the multiplication table of 5.

$$40 \div 5 = 8$$

$5 \times 8 = 40$

(b)

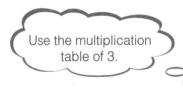

Use the multiplication table of 3.

$$3 \times 8 = 24$$

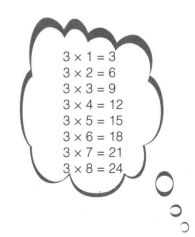

$3 \times 1 = 3$
$3 \times 2 = 6$
$3 \times 3 = 9$
$3 \times 4 = 12$
$3 \times 5 = 15$
$3 \times 6 = 18$
$3 \times 7 = 21$
$3 \times 8 = 24$

The weight of 3 boxes of fruit is [**24**] lb.

Solution to Question 70

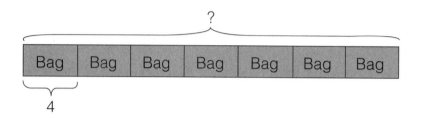

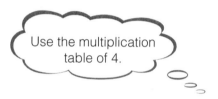

Use the multiplication table of 4.

$7 \times 4 = 28$

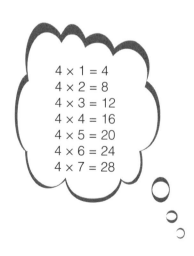

4 × 1 = 4
4 × 2 = 8
4 × 3 = 12
4 × 4 = 16
4 × 5 = 20
4 × 6 = 24
4 × 7 = 28

She picked [**28**] tomatoes.

Notes

Notes

Notes

Notes

Notes

Notes

Notes

Notes